Field Trips

At the Apple Orchard

By Sophie Geister-Jones

level 2 little blue readers

www.littlebluehousebooks.com

Little Blue House is distributed by North Star Editions:
sales@northstareditions.com | 888-417-0195

Produced for Little Blue House by Red Line Editorial.

Photographs ©: onepony/iStockphoto, cover; Nikada/iStockphoto, 4; Sophia_Apkalikov/iStockphoto, 7; paulacobleigh/iStockphoto, 9; phototropic/iStockphoto, 11; KatieDobies/iStockphoto, 12–13; DebraMillet/iStockphoto, 14 (top); Vevchic86/iStockphoto, 14 (bottom), 24 (bottom left); nndanko/iStockphoto, 17 (top), 24 (top left); chas53/iStockphoto, 17 (bottom); onebluelight/iStockphoto, 18; FatCamera/iStockphoto, 21 (top), 24 (bottom right); tacstef/iStockphoto, 21 (bottom), 24 (top right); monkeybusinessimages/iStockphoto, 23

Library of Congress Control Number: 2019908257

ISBN
978-1-64619-026-3 (hardcover)
978-1-64619-065-2 (paperback)
978-1-64619-104-8 (ebook pdf)
978-1-64619-143-7 (hosted ebook)

Printed in the United States of America
Mankato, MN
012020

About the Author

Sophie Geister-Jones likes reading, spending time with her family, and eating cheese. She lives in Minnesota.

Table of Contents

At the Apple Orchard

We take a field trip to the apple orchard.

We want to pick apples.

We see many apple trees.

The trees grow in lines.

The trees have
many apples.

apple tree

Apples come in
different colors.
They can be red, green,
or yellow.

We pick the apples off
the trees.
We gather them in
our arms.

Some apples are on
the ground.
We do not take
those apples.

Apple Everything

The orchard has a store.

The store sells many things.

We see candy apples.

The store sells apple pie
and apple juice.
They are both made
with apples.

apple pie

apple juice

Orchard Fun

We have fun at the

apple orchard.

We get our faces painted.

We also see animals at
the apple orchard.
We see kittens
and ducklings.

We take our apples home so that we can eat them. The apples taste good.

Glossary

apple pie

duckling

candy apples

kitten

Index